Don't Just Stand There

105 Years of Wisdom
from My Italian Grandmother

Jeff Paterson

DON'T JUST STAND THERE

Published by Cataract Books

First Printing: May 2013
Printed in the United States of America

First Edition: May 2013

ISBN-13: 978-0615810072
ISBN-10: 0615810071

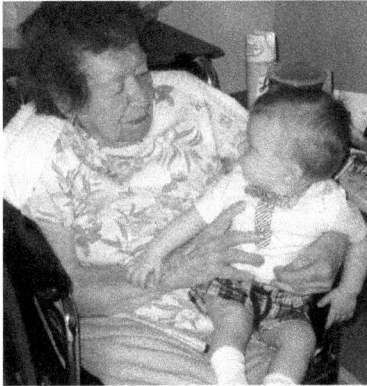

Dedicated to

Frances Genovese

and

Will Paterson

Contents

Acknowledgments

First and foremost, I want to thank my grandmother, Frances Genovese, for sharing her wisdom with all of us over these many years. I also thank my son, Will, who inspired me to capture this wisdom on paper.

Thanks to the love of my life, Michele, for encouraging me throughout this process and enduring months of watching me obsessively write and edit. Thanks also to my parents, Bill and Joan Paterson, for raising my brother and me to respect our elders, value our family history, and appreciate the power of language. Special thanks to my brother, Bill, his wife, Jenn, and their daughter, Katie, for their love and friendship. And thanks to Max, the ever-loveable cat who often curled up next to me and helped me with my typing.

Thanks to my father-in-law, Skip Long, who shares my interest in family history and patiently listened to me prattle on about this book while I was writing it. To my nieces and nephews, aunts and uncles, great aunts and uncles, cousins and extended family – living and deceased, in-laws and "outlaws" – my sincere gratitude for staying close and reminding me always of the importance of family.

Extra special thanks to those who shared their memories of Frances over the years by email and in person, namely Eleanor Cicero, Don DeBiase, Joe DeBiase, Joyce DeBiase, Pat DeBiase, Vinny DiFranco, Richard Jones and Shirley Monaco.

And to the faith community of St. John de LaSalle in Niagara Falls, where my grandmother is the oldest parishioner and my son is one of the youngest, thank you for being my second family.

Preface

Frances Genovese reading a card on her 95th birthday

1

Only about 54,000 Americans today are 100 or older. That's less than 0.02 percent of the nation's population.

My grandmother joined their ranks on June 9, 2008, an occasion that drew relatives from around the country to our hometown of Niagara Falls, New York. When I told friends that my grandmother was about to turn 100, many assumed that our family would be gathering around the bedside of someone who was barely conscious.

They never met Frances Genovese.

She entered her second century of life as sharp as a tack, still living in her own apartment. Standing less than five feet tall, with just one pound on her petite frame for each year of her life, she remained the formidable force that held our family together. She was a regular at family get-togethers, senior club meetings and Sunday Mass. She even had her own teeth.

My grandmother has had a few setbacks in the years since, but she still has her faculties – and her teeth! With her 105th birthday just around the corner, I just keep reflecting on this seemingly ordinary woman's extraordinary life.

*

My grandfather died in 1991 at the age of 87. My grandmother was 83 at the time, and I was 15. I guess my grandfather's death made me reflect, because it suddenly occurred to me for the first time that Frances wouldn't be around forever. I realized that we needed to record her stories and memories for posterity. I bought her a fill-in-the-blanks personal history book so she could put everything in writing. She never used it. For her, the joy of stories is in the telling. So I resolved to start jotting down her stories when she told them. But years went by and I still hadn't written a thing.

As Frances's 100th birthday drew near, I had to admit that time wasn't on our side. It was time to get started. I took my laptop to my grandmother's apartment a few times and recorded hours of conversations with her during the weeks leading up to the big birthday celebration. I also invited relatives near and far to share their favorite remembrances and dug up email recollections that had swirled around a few years earlier.

All of these memories, taken together, formed a narrative of Frances Genovese's life, set against the backdrop of her family's Italian American story of tenacity and perseverance. This material became the basis for a short book on Frances's life. Every guest at her 100th birthday party received a copy.

Four years later, I decided to reshape the book into a new format for a whole new purpose.

*

Our son, Will, was born on September 5, 2012. It astonishes me to think that Will is held, week after week, by someone 104 years older than he is. But in all likelihood, he won't get to know Frances as well as the rest of us have. He may not have a chance to learn the life lessons that we have absorbed from her.

This book began as an attempt to pass my grandmother's wisdom on to Will. At some point I realized that other people might also be interested in a 105-year-old's perspectives on life. So here we are.

Some of the 15 lessons in this book are direct quotes from my grandmother. Others are drawn from her example. Either way,

Frances's wisdom has helped me to make some sense of a nonsensical world. I hope it will help my son – and maybe it will help you, too.

1

Don't Just Stand There

Frances on one of her many trips

On December 12, 2001, at the age of 93, Frances Genovese walked into Fleet Bank on North Military Road in Niagara Falls, as she had so many times before. She was doing some routine banking while her eldest daughter, Marie, waited in the car.

According to a newspaper account, "Robbers entered wearing black ski masks, white latex gloves and had guns. They were yelling and demanding money. Everyone, customers and bank employees, knew the bank was being robbed."

The robbers told everyone to stay put. But Frances calmly walked out, went to the car and told Marie to call 911. Frances's youngest daughter, Joan, asked her later why she had left the bank when she could have been shot.

Frances replied, "I didn't want to be there, so I just went out the door. I don't know why everybody just stood there."

*

There's an Italian proverb that says, "Who moves, picks up. Who stands still, dries up." By that standard, Frances Genovese has never been in danger of drying up, because she has never stood still for very long.

Fran sums up the first 27 years of her life in a refrain that most of her family can recite from memory: "I was born in Shawmut, Pennsylvania, I made my first communion in Corry, Pennsylvania, I made my confirmation in New Castle, Pennsylvania, and I got married in Niagara Falls."

The wherewithal to keep moving was a gift from her immigrant parents and grandparents.

*

Frances Mary DeBiase was born on June 9, 1908, to Donato and Vincenza (Giovanelli) DeBiase. Both Donato and Vincenza came from the farming town of Troia in the province of Foggia, situated in the Puglia region of southern Italy.

The brother of a priest, Donato had spent time in the seminary in Italy. But when his godfather came to America, Donato decided to

8

follow him. Donato landed in Crenshaw, a small mining town in northwestern Pennsylvania. Meanwhile, Vincenza was living in nearby Shawmut, an even tinier mining town just a few miles away. The two met and later married, on Christmas Day 1905.

"It's funny," Frances says. "They were all from the same town in Italy, and they all landed in the same area in Pennsylvania."

When Frances was a little girl, her family picked up and moved to Corry, a larger city near the northwest tip of Pennsylvania. Donato was foreman for the construction of a new post office there. The family also had a grocery store in the building where they lived. "Mom ran the store, then Dad took over when he got home from work," Frances recalls.

The ever-expanding clan moved again in 1915, this time to New Castle, located on the western Pennsylvania border very close to Youngstown, Ohio. Donato had a bakery there, and he delivered his bread to stores and homes using a horse named Dutch, and later a Model-T truck. Next he owned a coal yard, where Frances worked as the secretary.

New Castle was home for 11 years, and life was good for a while. "We had a lot of money in New Castle," Frances's sister Eleanor recalled in an email decades later. But, like so many others, the family soon tasted hardship.

"Depression came early to New Castle when all the factories left town," Eleanor recalled. "One day a relative came to visit from Niagara Falls. He said there was plenty of work there – so we moved our family to Niagara Falls."

It was 1926. Frances was on her fourth hometown and her second state. She was 18.

"When we came to Niagara Falls, I didn't come with my parents," she remembers. "I was working. I had given notice, and so I had to keep working the following week." She stayed with her grandparents in New Castle and made the trip to Niagara Falls a week later with some family friends.

Donato and Vincenza eventually had 11 surviving children, of whom Frances was the eldest. The DeBiases moved several times over the years, always within the confines of Niagara Falls. Donato took a factory job, which he tolerated because it kept his family fed.

But he didn't enjoy it.

Fran started working in the office at the Carborundum plant, where she met a young man named Anthony Genovese. Tony and Fran became part of a large social group that enjoyed vaudeville acts, dancing and big band music. The oldest DeBiase brother, Jim, was the chaperone.

Frances and Tony married in September 1935 and settled into a two-story house on 63rd Street in the LaSalle section of Niagara Falls. LaSalle had been its own village until 1927, when it was annexed by the city. Unlike the city proper, LaSalle's neighborhoods were not organized along ethnic lines and had a suburban feel. There, Fran and Tony raised three daughters: Marie, Antoinette and Joan. Nine grandchildren followed: Julie, Kathy, William, Lori, Lynne, David, Steven, William and yours truly.

The 63rd Street house remained the family homestead for 54 years, but even during those stable years Frances never exactly stood still. She kept moving in new ways, including her work life.

*

Frances almost always worked outside the home. After she left Carborundum, she took jobs at a grocery store called Grizanti's and later at a men's store called Wallens. Her next and last stop was Beir's department store in downtown Niagara Falls, where she worked in the office.

"That was enough!" she says. "Tony retired in March 1969, and I worked until the end of September. He wanted to go to Florida, and I thought that was a good time for me to quit."

Fran didn't retire to sit in a rocking chair. It was the lure of travel that made her give up working. In their retirement, Tony and Fran saw sights all over North America – to the chagrin of Frances's mother. "She expected her daughters to be on call whenever she needed anything," Fran's daughter Joan remembers. "Once when I went to my parents' house to help them get ready for a trip, my mother was dreading making that phone call. She said, 'I'm 65 years old and I'm still afraid to tell my mother I'm going on vacation.'"

In 1980, Tony and Fran joined 10 others in founding the St. John de LaSalle Senior Citizens' Club at church. As the group grew, Fran became the travel coordinator. Willie Nelson's song "On the Road

Again" made it big that year. It became Tony and Fran's unofficial theme song just as quickly. They took so many trips – including her favorite, a voyage to Nova Scotia – that family members took to singing "On the Road Again" every time Fran announced a new expedition.

My grandparents' trip to Italy in 1980 marked Frances's first time on an airplane. She had a chance to see her parents' hometown and the family farm while she was in the old country. More about that later.

Once my grandfather's worsening dementia made it impossible to live safely in a home with stairs, he and my grandmother sold the house in 1989 and moved into a charming, spacious mobile home just a few miles away. Their travels together were over. Just getting out of the house was the most exotic trip Frances would make for the next two years. She relied on family, as well as volunteers from a community agency, to stay with my grandfather so she could go grocery shopping and take the occasional break from caregiving.

After Tony died in 1991, Frances took a little time to gather her thoughts, and then she was ready to hit the road again. The trips weren't as frequent, but they went on.

My grandmother went to New York City with a church group in the mid-1990s. They walked for hours, shopping and taking in the sights, and found themselves dreading the walk back to the hotel. Not to worry. Frances herded them all, most much younger, onto a bus and got them safely back to their rooms. They still talk about how the octogenarian saved the day.

She made another trip to Europe when she was well into her 80s, visiting several western European countries, including a second visit to Italy.

Frances tagged along with me when I went to Chicago in 2000, because her youngest sister and two of her brothers lived in the area. The highlight of the trip was a mini-reunion with 50 doting relatives all gathered around the family's undisputed matriarch.

My parents, my brother and sister-in-law and I flew to Arizona four years later to visit Eleanor's branch of the family. Frances joined us and, at age 95, was able to reconnect with more relatives she hadn't seen in a long time. We took a side trip to Las Vegas to see Uncle Donald in his new home. Fran brought along a few quarters so she could stop at a casino. She called it quits on the gambling the minute she ran out of quarters.

Frances took her last flight that summer, at age 96. Her beloved brother Joe had died, and more than 40 of us descended on the nation's capital for his burial at Arlington National Cemetery. In retrospect, it may not have been such a great idea for a bunch of Italians who hadn't seen each other in years to stage a reunion on a sightseeing trolley. We were shushed so many times by the other passengers that we finally got off the bus and started walking to all the sights. Fran was with us every step of the way as we trekked all over Washington and Arlington for two days, all in memory of Uncle Joe.

As time wore on and arthritis and a fractured hip took their toll, Fran had to give up traveling. But even at her advanced age, she didn't just stand there.

*

Day to day, past the age of 100, Frances Genovese would get up in the morning, make her toast and coffee, read the newspaper and straighten her apartment. She followed the news faithfully and always had plenty of opinions about what was happening in the world. Because I lived a few streets away, we shared a polling place and had a long-running tradition of voting together. She kept a standing appointment with the hairdresser. She socialized with friends and spent lots of time with family.

Fran came down with a nasty case of shingles just before Christmas 2005. But on Christmas Eve and Christmas Day, she still went from party to party and never complained, even though we could see the pain on her face. She wanted to be where the action was. It was Christmas, after all.

*

I had been dating my future wife for less than a year when Frances's 100th birthday gala rolled around. This was Michele's first chance to meet much of my local extended family, not to mention the dozens of out-of-state relatives.

How did Michele endear herself to my big Italian family? When it came time to clean up, she got up and helped. That's what they all remarked on after the party – that Michele didn't just stand there, but rolled up her sleeves and pitched in.

In Frances's world, "don't just stand there" also means "don't expect other people to wait on you." Frances would always get up after dinner to help clear the table. At age 93, she visited my newly purchased bachelor pad for dinner. I invited her to stay at the table after dinner and let me clean up. She ignored me and gave my sink and kitchen counters the best scrubbing they had ever seen.

*

Sometimes we have to keep moving because life demands it. Economic turmoil, new jobs and financial challenges forced Fran and her family to move around quite a bit in the early years. My grandfather's illness made it necessary to move on in the later years.

Sometimes we choose to keep moving because there's something more to see or do. The allure of travel and adventure kept Fran "on the road again" for much of her later life.

Sometimes we force ourselves to keep moving, even at the risk of our comfort, because we don't like what is happening around us. Bank robbers got Fran moving on a December day; for us it might be a situation at work that challenges our ethics, or a distasteful remark that offends our sensibilities, that tells us it's time to hit the road.

And sometimes, we get moving simply because there's work to do.

The common denominator is a sense of grit determination that stares down any self-doubt or inertia. We can't let complacency or anxiety about the unknown force us to stay still when something else awaits us.

Whatever makes us pick up our feet, we have to concede the basic truth that life is precious, and time is short, and when the going gets tough, you can't just stand there.

2

Remember Where You Came From

Frances's grandparents, Ben and Rose Giovanelli

Frances often talks about the way her family observed Lent. The DeBiases have always been faithful Catholics – especially my great-grandfather. In the 40 days leading up to Easter, Donato would lock up the family's player piano to add a note of solemnity to the season. "We weren't allowed to go to movies during Lent," Fran remembers, "and we were very strict about not eating meat on Friday *and* Wednesday."

The mood brightened when Lent gave way to Easter. Her mother, Vincenza, would buy a bolt of cloth to make Easter dresses for the girls and shirts for the boys. Vincenza would spread all the baked goods out on the dining room table, and the priest would visit the house to bless them all. After Easter Mass, the family would dine on a fattened lamb. A big basket stood on the table with candy and straw, and there was always extra Easter bread to be shared with extended family and friends.

By repeating these stories, Fran reminds us about the importance of religious feasts and family holidays. Storytelling is a big part of her job in our family. It's how she links the present to the past.

*

Some of Fran's reverence for family history came from her relationship with her maternal grandparents, Urbano (known as "Ben") and Rose (Capone) Giovanelli. Unlike her father's parents, whom she never met, the Giovanellis came to the United States and lived nearby.

"Grandpa was real tall and Grandma was short," Fran recalls. "And he was always so cute. He'd always call her 'Rosalina,' and he'd pat her on the head and put his arm around her. He was always really nice with everybody, always joking. We were really close with Grandma and Grandpa because we lived in the same town."

According to Frances, Ben was a shoemaker and Rose was "just a sweet person, very nice." The couple added an old world flavor to the family.

"Grandma made her own bread and her own macaroni all her life," says Fran. "She never bought any. She always baked. And Grandpa used to bake beautiful cakes. He baked my cousin Connie's wedding cake. He used to be a cook when he was in Italy, and he loved cooking."

21

Sometimes the language barrier provided comic relief. "All of my cousins in Pennsylvania knew Grandma Rose liked ginger ale, and she called it 'gingianelle.' So we always called it that. And one time my grandfather was repairing shoes, and this man said, 'How long do you guarantee them?' He said, 'Till they's broke.' And that was something the kids always talked about."

Frances and her grandmother formed a special bond during those years. "She'd always take me to go shopping with her because she couldn't speak English very well," says Fran. "So when we got through, she'd buy me a pair of anklets. It was ten cents a pair."

Grandpa Ben and Grandma Rose connected my grandmother to life in Italy, and to bygone traditions that they learned from previous generations. Today, my grandmother links my son and the other great-grandchildren to things that happened five generations ago and beyond. The great-grandkids will someday pass these stories on to their kids and grandkids – and in 2050, maybe someone yet to be born will pick up a glass of ginger ale and call it "gingianelle."

It's an amazing gift of continuity.

*

Frances has always been rooted in history, but her appreciation for family ties reached new heights when she visited Foggia in 1980. There she saw the family farm and met some of her long-lost relatives – all children and grandchildren of Urbano DeBiase, her father's eldest brother.

During Frances's visit, her cousins were thrilled to learn that each of her brothers bore the name of a DeBiase relative back in Italy. Frances's eldest brother, James, was named for his father, Donato, who took the name "James" when he came to the United States. John was named for Donato's brother, Giovanni, the priest. Patrick was named for Donato's father, Pasquale. Ben was named for Urbano. Louis and Joseph were named for Luigi and Giuseppe, two of Donato's uncles. And Donald was named for Donato, bringing the whole thing full-circle. Yes, family heritage played a big role – and yet, the names were Anglicized for a new time in a new land. Apparently, Frances's parents didn't stand still, either.

The feeling of continuity just kept unfolding during my grandmother's trip to the old country. In a subsequent letter to her brother Pat, Frances wrote, "Now I know why the DeBiase boys like big homes and a lot of land, because that is what they all have and what the family always had."

Today, my grandmother says of the family farm in Italy, "I don't know, I just felt comfortable there." She put it even more strongly back in 1980: "I felt as though I'd been there before – a strange feeling."

"When you went in, the steps were the most beautiful marble," Frances told me recently. "I wanted to take one of them home. Everything was beautiful – the furniture and everything – and it was really big. They had grapevines and olive trees, and there was a big room with big barrels of wine, and another room where they made olive oil. They sold the wine and oil. They had all kinds of fruit and herbs – patches and patches of them – and lambs. They had their own chapel there. They had Mass on Sundays and holy days for the workers. They were very religious."

She left Foggia in awe of her father's sacrifices. "I always wondered why my father left Italy," she says. "Where he came from in Italy, they were very well off. The people who knew the family never called him Donato. They called him 'Don Donato.'"

Social and political forces probably figured into Donato's decision to leave his country. There's a cultural divide between northern and southern Italians. At the turn of the 20th century, the Italian government was controlled by northerners, who imposed high taxes and tariffs that were making it harder and harder to earn a good living in the south. So, Don Donato gave up a comfortable life that threatened to grow uncomfortable. He grabbed onto the unshakeable faith that the future would be better in America.

In Italy, he was educated and respected. In the States, he died prematurely, heartbroken after sending his sons to fight in foreign lands. But his children and their children and grandchildren have made a great life here. They've been elected to office and run corporations and taught children and raised families and served their churches and proudly worn the country's uniform in battle.

Donato's struggles were a down payment on his family's future. We're aware of that because my grandmother and her brothers and sisters have kept the story alive. By doing so, they've reminded us that we have an obligation to honor our ancestors' sacrifices by being the best we can be.

That's the key to honoring the past, Frances Genovese-style. You don't wallow in it or dwell on it. Instead, you create new stories on top of the old ones. You use your heritage as a compass to point you toward the future.

These words, often attributed to Cicero, hold a great deal of wisdom: "Who knows only his own generation remains always a child." If you've never asked your parents, grandparents, aunts and uncles to tell you their stories, don't wait any longer. They're your stories, too.

3

Cherish Education

Frances with the author at his 1993 high school graduation

In the late 1970s, Fran bought savings bonds for the youngest grandchildren – "because I might not live long enough to see them graduate, and I want them to have a little something." Fortunately, she has lived long enough to see all of us – and, more recently, the six oldest great-grandchildren – finish high school. There have been lots of college graduations, too.

As the youngest of Frances's nine grandchildren, I was the last to graduate from high school. It was June 1993, and she had just turned 85. I remember her palpable sense of relief that she was able to be there.

Around that time, my mother mentioned that Frances had always loved graduations. I never understood why until recently, when my grandmother told me about her own educational journey.

"My mother didn't want me to go to high school," Frances Genovese told me, as if the memory were fresh. "All the neighbor kids were working at 15, and that's all I ever heard. She'd say, 'You should go to work at the pottery like all the other kids in the neighborhood. But no, you have to go to school.'"

Fran's father always stood up for her. "You want to go to school?" he'd ask. "You go to school!"

For Donato, formal schooling was a priority. Having studied at the seminary in the old country, he had an innate sense of the value of education. "He was always proud whenever someone finished school," Fran recalled. No wonder he insisted that his older daughter finish high school. And no wonder she feels the way she does about graduation ceremonies.

*

Another reason Fran cherishes education is that she had to work extra hard for hers.

"In New Castle," Fran says, "downtown is lower but everything else is up on a hill. In the winter, you couldn't walk up because it was slippery. They had a great big rope that was tied to a big pole. And you just hung on to that all the way up till you got to the top."

New Castle had one high school, which all the students attended no matter where they lived. "Most everyone walked to school," says Fran. "We had trolleys then – just streetcars – and it was only five cents. So the people who lived real far took the streetcar in. I did sometimes when it was late or the weather was real bad. Otherwise, I walked because I didn't have too far to walk to where we went up the hill."

Young Fran wasn't encouraged to stay after school for activities. "If I did, I'd get bawled out because I had to get home to help," she says. Still, she pushed the envelope because she wanted to expand her skills. "There was a course in home nursing," she recalls, "and I wanted to take it, but you had to stay after school for an hour after class for half a year, and I always got home late. But I did it."

Fran graduated from high school at 16 because she had an early start. "Back then there was no kindergarten," she says. "You went right to first grade. I was 5 years old, so my parents just told them I was 6. So I graduated on June 3, 1925, and I turned 17 on June 9." (Yes, she still remembers the exact date of her high school graduation.)

The family had a simple reason for accelerating Frances's education. With all those brothers and sisters at home, she had to finish school as quickly as possible so she could get a job and help with household chores.

Vincenza may not have wanted her daughter to attend school, but both parents were pleased when graduation day finally came. Fran's sister Eleanor recalled that "Mama and Papa were so proud they bought Fran a gold wristwatch and let her pick out the dress she wanted in our very best store!"

Frances had achieved a major goal – and in the process, she made education a top priority for the whole family.

4

Keep Your Door Open

The homestead on 63rd Street in Niagara Falls

One of Frances's nephews, Vinny DiFranco, has great memories of my grandparents' house on 63rd Street. As a teenager, Vinny worked at the Grand Bowling Alley at the end of the street.

"When I see a bowling alley," he wrote in 2000, "I think of the number of times I stopped by my Aunt Fran's house to eat when I got a break from setting pins. Someone was always stealing my lunch that my mother had packed. When you are 15 you get hungry."

My grandparents' house later became a regular stop for Vinny because of its proximity to the bus stop at the edge of Niagara Falls. "When I see a young man get off a Greyhound bus," he wrote, "I think of my treks when I got off a similar bus with a Greyhound logo. Depending on which time in my life, I would either have my dirty laundry from college or my Army duffle bag. I would walk to her house and be greeted by that great smell of sauce and a hearty hug. From there she would hand me off to my mother and father."

*

For both sides of the extended family, the house on 63rd Street was part hotel, part restaurant and part Grand Central Station for decades. That spirit of hospitality was something Frances acquired as a child.

During the prosperous years, the DeBiase family lived in a 10-room house at 26 Beaver Street in New Castle, with six rooms downstairs divided by a long hallway that led to a square patio and out the back door. The house was always open to visitors, including a boy from the local orphanage. "Pa made sure he had a hot meal on Sundays," Fran's sister Eleanor later remembered.

Frances continued the open-door policy once she was married with a house of her own. Many relatives lived with her at one time or another. Eleanor moved in when her husband lost his job; in fact, they were living with Fran when their son, Vinny from the bowling alley, was born. Vinny always said that the house on 63rd Street was "his house," because that's where he landed when he got out of the hospital as a newborn.

Fran's sister Evelyn stayed for a while when she and her husband, Dave, sold their house and had to wait for the new one to be ready. Brother Jim and his family stayed after a fire damaged their home.

Tony's sister Stella stayed when her husband, Jerry, was in the service. "She didn't want to be home alone," Fran explains.

Fran's youngest brother, Don, also stopped by from time to time. "There's about 30 years between us," says Don. "We lived in downtown Niagara Falls, and she lived across town in LaSalle, and none of us drove. So we really didn't see each other very much. But when I was going to Bishop Duffy High School and playing football, the coach sometimes would call a chalkboard session at night. It was a couple of miles from Fran's house, so I would walk over and have dinner and then go back to the chalk session."

Her hospitality extended beyond the house. Great nephew Richard Jones still remembers visiting Fran when she was working at the Wallens men's store. "Every Tuesday we had church school," he recalls. "It was a long walk home. On cold winter days we would always stop and see Aunt Fran at Wallens. Inside Wallens, they had a gum machine which had the little slide handle where you put in the penny and got two Chiclet-type pieces of gum for your penny. Aunt Fran would always buy us a piece of gum and say that it was good for us because we kept warmer by chewing it on our way home, keeping our jaws moving."

*

As the family scattered across the country and around the world, the house on 63rd Street became Niagara Falls headquarters – a regular stop for all visitors. Brother Lou's wife, Rose, and their children stayed for a month while Lou worked in Panama. Brother Pat's wife, Joyce, also stayed at various times – shortly after she married Pat, and later when she used to take their daughter Debbie back and forth to school in Connecticut.

"Boiling it down to one memory," Joyce wrote several years ago, "I'd have to choose three days in April in the year 1947. It was then that Fran took me to the Easter Triduum at St. Mary's Church down by the Falls: Holy Thursday, Good Friday, Holy Saturday. Sitting there in awe of the liturgies presented, I experienced a leap of faith more powerful than anything I had ever experienced before. Even though I had been brought up close to the faith as a Protestant, this was an overwhelming experience. Those three days were the beginning of my conversion to Catholicism. For this I am eternally grateful."

Most memorably for the rest of us, Fran's brother Joe stayed with her whenever he visited – which was often, and sometimes unannounced. All of us looked forward to Uncle Joe's visits, because he was a fascinatingly free spirit who could talk at length on any subject, from sports to geopolitics to bituminous coal, without a hint of pretense. And he always brought interesting gifts, including books, toys and even secondhand clothes.

Once, Joe arrived with two South American women who wanted to visit nearby Canada. "They had dinner at our house," Fran remembers. "They were real friendly and they gave me a bottle of perfume and a silk scarf." She kept that perfume for decades, until the last drop was gone.

Even after my grandfather died and my grandmother was living in the mobile home, she readily shared her spare room with visitors – especially Joe. He arrived one fall in an absurdly huge powder blue Cadillac that filled the driveway. He enjoyed meeting up with his childhood friends, though these outings sometimes left Joe suffering the next day. "Joe never learned that Jack Daniel's is a sipping whiskey," his friend Walt Dean once told me.

It wasn't easy for Frances to sleep when Joe was around. Having been a prisoner of war, he could never stand to be confined. He'd get up constantly during the night for snacks, and then his stomach would be upset, so he'd have a hard time going back to sleep.

Sometimes he would go outside for air in the middle of the night. He'd slip off to McDonald's at the crack of dawn and befriend the old codgers drinking coffee. When he returned, the slamming door would wake Frances all over again.

She loved having him nonetheless. "Sometimes now I feel bad around the holidays," she says, "because I think Joe should be visiting. It just doesn't feel right not to have him around."

*

Just as Frances's house belonged to her extended family, it also belonged to all of us grandkids. It was our second home. Our pictures adorned the wall along the staircase to the second floor. We were always welcome for sleepovers, dinners and visits, and there were lots of memorable items and places in the house.

There was the old record player in the dining room, complete with a collection of vinyl LPs. (I especially loved the Frank Sinatra records. I can still remember sitting in front of that magic machine, listening to Frank croon, "A quarter to three … there's no one in the place except you and me.") There were the glass canning jars lined up in the basement, along with my grandfather's workshop, where he liked to build things. There was the sight of my grandfather cracking nuts and playing solitaire at the kitchen table. Of course, there was always food. And there was everyone's favorite spot: the front porch, where we would play games, talk to the neighbors and watch the world go by.

The porch was where Grandpa gave each of us his famous lecture about the evils of smoking. "When I was 6 years old," he would intone with utter solemnity, "my brother handed me a stogie and told me to try it. I got so sick, I never smoked a stogie again. I don't ever want you to smoke." We were pretty sure that if we did start smoking, he would find out and kill us long before the cigarettes had a chance to.

When we visited their house, my grandfather would inevitably drift away into his recliner, where he would sit and watch his Yankees. But my grandmother made us feel like we were the most important people in the world. She always seemed happy to see us. And to this day, Frances lights up when any of us stops by to say hello.

*

The fall of 2010 was tough for Frances. She landed in the hospital on September 11 with congestive heart failure. She returned home weak, and it was hard for her to go out. She spent the winter months confined to her apartment. Visits from the family kept her going.

With some struggle, she was able to get out on Christmas Day. But Christmas Eve was out of the question, because she couldn't be out two days in a row. So we decided to hold our Christmas Eve celebration in her small apartment. Under Fran's direction, everyone brought food and extra chairs, and more than 20 of us packed into her place. It was congested, but it was fun – and it meant the world to her. For that brief moment, she relived the joy of the Christmases when her house was the center of the universe.

*

Most kids have a home away from home. It might be a best friend's house, a neighbor's house or a relative's house, but it's a special place – a place that's warm and welcoming. Frances's house was that place for us grandkids and for countless others. It was kind of like the Motel 6: Frances would leave the light on for whoever might stop by.

Recently, as she reflected on the constant traffic that went through those hallways, my grandmother put it succinctly: "It was everybody's house." And she was everyone's mother and grandmother by extension.

What a great reminder to keep our doors open, to make our homes warm and inviting.

*

When she turned 100, Frances couldn't believe that any of the family would come from around the country. She was amazed when more than 100 relatives representing every branch of the family, including her in-laws, turned up for the celebration. I think they came because of those many years of hospitality. She had opened her home and her heart to all of them for decades. They just wanted to return the favor.

5

Food Equals Love

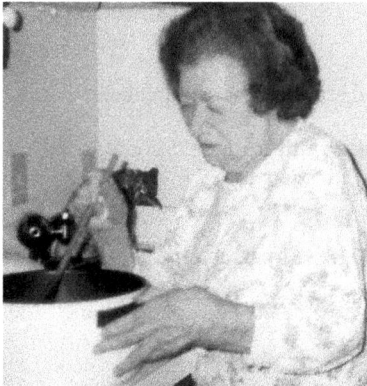

Frances in the kitchen

One of the best Christmas presents I've ever received was homemade. My mother painstakingly prepared a cookbook filled with favorite family recipes, pictures and stories. My brother and sister-in-law got one, too.

When I make a pot of sauce – something we were trained to do when my mom held a special "sauce class" for us – I feel connected to generations gone by. It's hard to ignore the fact that relatives I never even knew once entered into these same rituals and made these same foods. That's why I keep three pictures on the wall of my kitchen: one of my mother, one of my grandmother, and one of my great-grandmother. Somehow, I am united with them when I'm cooking.

*

In our family, as in most Italian families, hospitality means food, and food means love. We serve something when we want someone to feel welcome. If someone visits near the dinner hour, we fret about whether the person has eaten, and we usually end up

43

preparing some food just in case. If it's after dinner, we offer cookies – pizzelles always go over well – or nuts or fruit or whatever else we may have. We always try to keep something on hand, just in case. In fact, my mother and Aunt Marie both baked cookies for us to serve to unexpected visitors after our son was born.

Frances has always been quick to offer – some might say force-feed – refreshments to visitors.

When her brother Lou was going to Niagara University after the war, he and his friend Bruno worked on the college newspaper. They went to a print shop in Buffalo once a week to pick up their handiwork.

"They had to go by my house," says Fran, "so they'd stop for coffee, and I always had something ready for them. So this one day, I was late, and I made a pie but it was still hot. We had a milk box that the milkman would put the milk in. So I opened that and put the pie in it to cool off."

Lou and Bruno arrived and sat at the kitchen table, and Fran poured coffee for them. "Then I went to get the pie," she says with a hearty laugh, "and there was no pie there. I said, 'Oh my God, I put a pie there to get cool. Someone must have taken it.' Well, he and Bruno burst out laughing. They had taken it and hidden it."

There are two key points to this story. First, my grandmother always prepared food for her brother and his friend, week in and week out. And second, Uncle Lou and Bruno used her food to create laughter and memories. My grandmother still tells this story today, more than 60 years after the great pie caper took place.

Much later in life, when my grandmother wasn't cooking or baking as much, she took to serving packaged cookies or canned fruit to visitors. She still had to offer something.

My brother hates canned pineapple. He would turn it down under almost any circumstances. But when my grandmother gave it to him on one particular visit, he ate it with a smile on his face. No one had the heart to say no to Granny's food. That was her saying "I love you" – and you said it back by eating what she served you.

*

If you come from Italian stock, you're familiar with what I call "The Curse of the Surplus." We live in eternal fear of bringing shame on our family by running out of food. Part of this is psychology. If there's just enough for everyone, the guests won't eat as much as they want, because no one wants to take the last of anything. So we always cook for more people than we're expecting. It's a catastrophe even to come close to running out of food.

For us, food speaks as loudly as words when it comes to showing love. That's why Italians are known for pushing food on people. It's how we express care and friendship.

This may seem to be an unhealthy attitude. Isn't it dangerous to put food on such a pedestal, especially in an era when obesity is skyrocketing? Quite the opposite. My grandmother has taught us that food is sacred, even sacramental. After all, Jesus used bread and wine to set the pattern for the way his followers still worship today. If you view it in that way – a divine gift that conveys love – then food is something to be treasured and not abused.

My grandmother eats and drinks in moderation. Weight has never been a problem for her. I believe it's because food occupies a balanced position in her life. It's too special a thing to be mistreated. My grandmother has always sent food when someone close to the family dies. It's a tangible way to show concern. The family of the

46

deceased will be busy taking care of other things, and people will be showing up to offer their condolences. All of these people have to eat, so it's only right to send food.

During the Buffalo-Niagara area's infamous Blizzard of 1977, my grandparents were stuck inside for two days after barely making it home from the grocery store. Lou's wife, Rose, was being treated at the time at Roswell Park Cancer Institute in Buffalo, and Lou was stuck there because of the weather. Fran and her brother Jim decided to take Jim's truck out into the snow-piled streets for a 40-mile round trip to visit Lou at the hospital.

"I was making sauce," Frances recalls, "so I thought, 'I'm going to make some meatball sandwiches and take them to Lou. He probably hasn't had anything to eat.' So I made sandwiches and I wrapped them all up so they'd stay warm. And he was so happy." With a belly full of meatballs, Lou was finally able to get back home to Poughkeepsie the next morning.

My grandmother was active with our church's Marthas group, which puts on bereavement luncheons after parish funerals, until she was no longer physically able to do it. For many years, Frances made the phone calls to line up volunteers and find out what they would be making. Even after she gave that up, she could still be counted on to make her signature rice and broccoli casserole, or maybe a fresh batch of pizzelles. For Frances, food is a ready salve for the wounds that life inflicts.

*

There was a priest in Buffalo who used to take pizza and chicken wings to local police stations to thank the cops for their work. He was known for showing up on the scene with food when there was an accident or some other catastrophe. He even organized a parish drive to send pizzas to flooding victims in the next county over.

"I'm half Italian," he told a newspaper reporter, "and I try to Italianize the world through food. You can never have enough food."

*

It's no coincidence that some of my grandmother's favorite stories relate to food. In fact, she can still picture herself back in New Castle, nearly a century ago, enjoying a beloved childhood treat. Her family was lucky enough to have an ice cream factory across the street. "At night, they'd pick up all the empty containers of ice cream from different stores," says Frances. "They'd sit us all along the edge and give us the extra ice cream. Then on Sunday, that was our treat. We used to buy a brick of ice cream."

Later, as a young wife and mother, Frances decided to try something new. When the farmer came to deliver eggs and vegetables one day, Fran bought a live chicken. "I tried to kill it," she says with a laugh, and the poor thing just hobbled around." As my Aunt Anne remembers it, the chicken was "flapping around the cellar with my mother screaming after it." Tony had to put the bird out of its misery when he got home from work. Fran recalls, "He told me, 'Don't you ever buy a live chicken again!' But it tasted good."

Good food was a responsibility that Frances shared with her daughters, who were all expected to pitch in. Because she was a working mother, she looked to the three girls to help with dinner. Besides, the family recipes had to be passed on. Aunt Marie remembers "waking up Sunday morning to the sound of the big rolling pin flapping the perfect circle of ravioli dough and knowing I had to seal them all."

Canning season was an annual event of epic proportions. The whole family worked for hours and days at a time to can fresh tomatoes, peaches, pears and beans for later use. The tomatoes were especially challenging. Once they were cooked, they went into hanging cloth bags so the water would drain from them; after a few days, the tomatoes were ready to be canned. Sure, it was a lot of work, but it allowed the family to enjoy locally grown fruits and vegetables all year long. And it created memories that are still shared today.

*

Shortly after I moved out of my parents' house and bought my own place, my grandmother gave me a stock pot for making sauce, along with a bulb of garlic and a set of wooden spoons. I've used the pot extensively, and the garlic is long since gone. But I've never been able to bring myself to open that package of wooden spoons.

You understand the sanctity of wooden spoons if you're Italian. They're an essential tool for making sauce, preparing soup and even mixing ricotta for ravioli and manicotti and lasagna. When you have a good wooden spoon, you don't replace it until it's worn out. It's part of the family.

I don't can fruits and vegetables, but I do have my own tradition when it comes to making sauce. I use store-bought tomato puree as the base for my homemade sauce during most of the year. But every September, I use a sieve to make a big pot of sauce from fresh tomatoes. That's one of my favorite days of the year.

I always cook and freeze some extra tomatoes at that time, and I save them until the middle of winter when fresh ingredients are scarce. Then in February or March, I use the frozen puree, made from the previous summer's fresh tomatoes, to create a batch of sauce that tastes bolder and fresher than the usual sauce. In the bleakness of winter, it serves as a nice reminder of summer. That's how I feel about the wooden spoons my grandmother gave me. Someday, when I don't have Frances with me anymore, I'll open that package of spoons and let them remind me of her.

*

The table has always had pride of place in our family. It's a place to talk about what's happening in everyone's life, a place to analyze current events, a place to build relationships with each other. Food – for some, nothing more than a biological necessity – is our gateway to a rich family life and the deepest of friendships.

6

In All Things, Moderation

Tony and Fran's wedding day in 1935 –
postponed because of a bridesmaid's summer plans

When Frances turned 100, the local newspaper ran a feature story about her and a small group of other centenarians in the community. The reporter predictably asked for the secret of her longevity. Her response was characteristically funny: "Everybody asks me and I say, 'I have no secret.' If I did, I would sell it and make money."

The newspaper came calling again when her 104th birthday rolled around. Frances was reluctant to participate at first, but finally she relented. Not long before the interview, my mother said to me, "They're going to ask what her secret is, and she's going to tell them she doesn't have one. But I know her secret: don't get too emotional about anything."

There's more than a kernel of truth in what my mother said. Frances isn't given to extremes. When she's happy, she isn't deliriously happy. When she's angry, she isn't beside herself. When she's sad, she doesn't go down into the depths. There are no emotional roller coasters in Frances's life, and it seems to prevent much of the stress that can affect the more excitable among us.

*

My grandmother takes a moderate approach to most things. No matter how good a meal is, she stops when she's full. She might enjoy a glass of wine with dinner, but I've never seen her drink to excess. She wears nice clothes, but they're not extravagant. She enjoys chatting with people, but she isn't one to dominate a conversation. You name it – Frances doesn't overdo it.

Needless to say, not all of us are cut from this particular cloth. Some of us are born risk-takers and thrill-seekers. Some of us are highly emotional. Some of us have big appetites.

We don't have to change who we are. But my grandmother's example is a call to be mindful about how we approach life. Do we allow unnecessary drama in our lives, or are we too detached from the people around us? Are we too forgiving, or not forgiving enough? Do we need to be the center of attention, or are we too timid for our own good? Our worrying, our working, our spending, our loving, our complaining … do we do too much or too little of these things?

Every one of us is shaped by nature and nurture. Yes, we have certain tendencies that we don't necessarily choose, but ultimately we do have control over the choices we make. And there are worse places to be than the middle of the road.

Maybe she doesn't realize it, or maybe she just doesn't admit it, but that's my grandmother's secret.

*

My grandmother's "no extremes" policy especially applies to anger and grudges.

Frances fights back when she needs to. She's not afraid to stand up for herself when her core values are at risk. But most of the time, Frances keeps an even temper and works to maintain the peace. When she finds fault with someone, it is usually laced with pity. She has always said things like, "He must not be a very happy person," or "I wonder why she's like that – maybe she doesn't feel good." While she may dislike someone's behavior, she seldom, if ever, condemns the person.

Frances often says, "I don't understand why some families fight all the time. So you have a disagreement. You just have to let it go. It's not worth staying mad at people forever."

A prime example came from her wedding, held in September 1935. "We were supposed to get married at the end of August," Fran says. "Tony's sister was supposed to be in the wedding, but they had rented a cottage with a group through Labor Day. She said, 'We can't give up the cottage. We're not going to come back just for the wedding. The weekend is when we have more fun.'"

For a lot of brides, that would be an unforgiveable slight that might open a permanent rift. But my grandmother subtly reveals a path to forgiveness as she tells the story. First, she laughs about it. Her telling of the story doesn't drip with bitterness; she actually chuckles as she says it, as if to say, "Isn't that silly?"

Second, she tries to understand why it happened. In other words, she puts herself in her sister-in-law's shoes. "They wanted him to marry a woman named Angie – she was a good friend of theirs and they were always together," Fran says. "So naturally in their mind he was going to marry her."

And third, she finds an alternative. "We decided we'd move it to Labor Day," she says matter-of-factly. Rather than make the incident into a bitter conflict, she simply comes up with another approach that meets everyone's needs.

*

Most of us in the family aren't "my way or the highway" people. My grandmother has taught us to be tolerant of other people's opinions and to be respectful even when we don't exactly get our way. We've learned that it's good to fight when there's something worth fighting for, but sometimes compromise is the price of peace. It's important to know when to do battle – and there are times when you have to take a stand – and when to beat swords into plowshares.

Too much of either leads to an unbalanced life. For Frances, even anger happens in moderation.

7

There's Such a Thing as Duty

The DeBiase brothers at their father's funeral

Frances dealt with the challenges of rationing while raising a young family during World War II.

"I had a really nice neighbor," she recalls some 70 years later. "Her name was Mrs. Smith. It was just her and her husband, and they were kind of old. They'd always go out when the stores had butter, and she'd buy me a stick and bring it. She'd say, 'You've got children, and you need it. We don't have to have it.'"

These acts of kindness echoed my great-grandfather's generosity toward others. When he was still in business in New Castle, he tried to help people affected by the economic downturn. Donato just kept giving bread and coal to his clients until he was broke.

*

"I don't like this new world," Frances told me recently. "It's too selfish, too money-hungry. There isn't that closeness that there used to be with everybody, no matter who it was."

She may not use the exact words, but I think what my grandmother misses most is the sense of duty – the idea that we are all responsible for each other and for our world.

I can't blame her for finding something missing these days. Churches are struggling to pay their bills and maintain their ministries; many are closing altogether. Fraternal and service organizations are folding for a lack of members. Charitable organizations are having trouble raising money. Most neighborhoods aren't as close-knit as they used to be. Huge corporations driven by short-term profits are all too willing to abandon the workers and communities that have made them successful. Countless politicians stand ready to sell out their principles for the sake of the next election. Voters want balanced budgets but demand more government programs with no tax increases.

In a world warped by relentless marketing, we now look at every situation as a value proposition: what's in it for me? We're looking for a return on our investment. Sometimes it seems we're losing that old American idea, shaped by immigrants of all stripes, that there is such a thing as duty. Some things need to be done because they're right, whether or not there's an immediate payoff.

That's my grandmother's ethic.

You go to church not just to feel good or to have your problems fixed overnight. You go to give some praise to the God who created you, whether you "get something out of it" or not. Worship is not entertainment, but acknowledgment that there's something bigger than you in the universe.

You don't attend funerals and wakes for the fun of it. You go because a life well-lived merits a few minutes of your time, even if you'd rather be somewhere else.

You visit people in the hospital whether or not you enjoy the experience. You send cards when people are sick. You send food when someone dies. You volunteer your time for good causes. You donate money when you can. You don't do it for recognition or profit. You do it because that's what people have to do to keep the world running smoothly and humanely.

After all, it's not always about us. We all have a duty to something other than our own luxury and sense of entitlement. Our grandparents understood that duty.

*

As we've already seen, my grandmother was heavily influenced by her dad. "He had a lot of friends," she says proudly. "He was involved in politics and different Italian groups. He was always involved in something."

That included St. Vitus Church, which was the Italian church in New Castle. "If my father went to 10:00 Mass," she says, "he never got home until 1:00. He took up the collection and stayed to count the money. He never missed Mass, and we had to go to Mass, too."

Frances's involvement in church was a gateway to volunteering. "During World War I, we used to make scarves and blankets for the soldiers," she remembers. "I belonged to a group from church, and they'd give us the yarn, and that's how I learned to knit. And they had this huge flag, and they'd get kids from different schools. I was always one of the ones picked. There would be a bunch of kids who would hold this huge flag, and we'd march in the parade, and people would throw money in it, and that's how they made money. I was in a lot of parades."

When she was a little older, Fran touched many lives as a church school teacher. She started by helping at St. Mary's Church, which was near her house. Before long, she was asked to take on a different assignment in a neighborhood on the southwestern end of New Castle. "In Mahoningtown, they had an Italian priest and an Italian church," she recalls. "They wanted somebody who could talk to the people and understand what they were saying. So I was sent to Mahoningtown. I used to take a streetcar right after lunch. At that time it was Sunday school at 2:00 in the afternoon."

Fran's father encouraged her volunteer service. "My mother used to always say, 'You're always in something!' And my father would say, 'Let her go!' And that was it."

She was doing her duty, after all.

*

When she wasn't busy helping at church or in the community, Frances had her hands full at home.

"My mother was busy," Frances recalls. "She had 11 children to take care of, but we all helped. I was the oldest, so I had to help all of them. Once they were 2 or so, then I took care of them so she could be with the babies. I helped her raise all the kids. That's why I feel so bad whenever anything happens to any of them, because they were just like mine."

*

The family's devotion to duty was stretched to its limit once the United States entered World War II. Brother Jim DeBiase was married with a child and was considered too old for the draft, so he became an air-raid warden in charge of the area around Niagara Falls. Brother Ben joined the Army but was given a medical discharge because of his susceptibility to frostbite. The others had an appointment with destiny. One by one, John, Pat, Lou and Joe DeBiase went off to war.

When Lou became the third DeBiase son to be drafted, it cast a pall over the entire family. Donato took it especially hard. "He cried and cried," says Fran. Before Lou had even shipped out, his father had a heart attack, and died on January 5, 1943. Still close to home, Lou was able to attend the funeral – and Pat and John were given emergency leave.

"We all figured that my father had the heart attack because he had just said goodbye to his third son who he saw off to fight a war," Donald said in 2001.

Frances was a young mother then. "A lot of nights, I was afraid to go to bed," she says. "At that time, we never knew when there was going to be an alarm, and we had to have the lights out, so I had the card table in my bedroom so I could be with the kids, and I used to write letters to my brothers. Those were bad, bad years."

Joe soon followed his three brothers into combat. Meanwhile, Vincenza moved with the two youngest children, Mary Grace and Donald, into a smaller house. Once, the doorbell rang in the middle of the night, and Vincenza opened the door to hear an unfamiliar man say, "Western Union Telegram for Mrs. DeBiase."

"I opened the telegram and read it to my mother," Don recalls. "'This is to inform you that your son Pvt. Joseph DeBiase is missing in action.' My mother started yelling in Italian, cursing out President Roosevelt, the devil, and all mankind, for the war that took her sons away from her. We didn't get any more sleep that night."

"Later we got another visit from Western Union," says Don, who later served in Korea in his own right. "It was a telegram that informed us that Lt. John DeBiase was wounded in action. Again my mother cried and yelled and cursed out the world in her great Italian style. After some weeks or maybe months we were informed by the American Red Cross that Joe was a prisoner of war in Germany and John was in a hospital with part of his left leg missing. My mother, well, you know what her reaction was."

The war took a terrible toll on the family. The kids lost their father. Joe and the other boys lost their innocence. John lost a leg. All in the name of duty.

Little did they know that someone half a world away had been pulling for them during those difficult years. When Fran visited Italy, her cousins told her of Monsignor Giovanni DeBiase, the uncle she had heard so much about. During the war, he asked all the American GIs that he met if they knew any soldiers named DeBiase. A GI finally told the priest that he knew John DeBiase, and that John had lost a leg in combat. Monsignor DeBiase wanted to visit his nephew but was never able to find out where he was. "But," Frances wrote to her brother Pat after returning from Italy, "he said a Mass for Johnny and prayed daily that you would all get home safe."

They did – and having done their part to save the world from tyranny, they went to college on the GI Bill and scattered about the country to build families and careers. Life went on.

*

My grandmother learned another lesson about duty when my grandfather lost his job at Carborundum, not long after they were married. "I was lucky, because I was working in the office," says Fran, "but a lot of people got laid off."

A man appeared at the door one day asking for a donation for Catholic Charities. Fran said, "I'm sorry, I can't give you anything. My husband hasn't been working for three months now. I'd be very glad to help, but I can't."

The man handed a business card to her and said, "Tell him to go to the paper mill and show them this and tell them that I sent him there." He went, he was hired, and he worked at that mill until 1940, when he ended up at the Union Carbide plant.

My grandparents never forgot their benefactor. In fact, Frances still recalls that his name was Mr. Nolan. More importantly, she has donated to the annual Catholic Charities Appeal ever since. Catholic Charities helped her, and she feels a responsibility to repay the kindness three-quarters of a century later.

*

When my grandfather started going to an adult day care program in the late 1980s because of his dementia, Frances decided to volunteer at the agency. She helped out at the gift shop, selling handmade crafts that people had donated. She would sometimes take the bus across town just to be of service.

Joining church groups, starting her seniors' club, helping people in need … that's Frances Genovese. She always felt a sense of duty, like her father, to put other people's needs first.

8

Family Matters

Fran (bottom row, right) with all her brothers and sisters,
gathered around their mother (bottom row, center)

Joyce Garrett became Joyce DeBiase when she married Frances's brother Pat. It was certain heresy for Joyce, a Protestant southern belle, to marry an Italian Catholic Yankee. But she found herself embraced by her new sister-in-law.

"When Frances was 11 years old," Joyce wrote a few years ago, "she became my husband's second mother and for many siblings thereafter. Pat was always grateful for the role she played in his life. Each of us could write a book about her goodness. She makes all things better, from a skinned knee to broken dreams, and is the first to arrive when there is a need: by bus, train, car, plane or on foot, she's there."

"Whenever a baby was born (every two years)," Eleanor recalled, "Fran and I took it and loved it and washed and dressed it – we only gave it back to Mama to nurse."

*

"I used to come home from school," says Fran, "and my mother would have the ironing board set up and bushels of clothes to iron, and I had to do it."

"This one time," she continues, "I was about 10 or 11 years old, and all the kids were in the back yard playing. So I started to go out, but my mother said, 'Get the ironing done first.' I had to iron all the handkerchiefs and napkins. So I did a few, and I thought, 'I'll hurry up and get them done so I can go out to play.' Back then, you'd use two irons – you'd use one while the other was heating on the stove. When I picked the other one up, it was too hot. What did I know? I opened the spigot, and the steam burned my hand. My grandmother grabbed me and put oil on my hand and wrapped it up."

Frances never had much of a chance to be a kid. She bore a lot of responsibility at home – her family needed her. Throughout her life, fidelity to family has been a constant. But she has never resented everyone's need for her love and care. For Frances, family is the most important thing.

*

"Bigga family, bigga trouble," Vincenza DeBiase used to say. And her eldest daughter was the family's number-one troubleshooter.

"Frances made the most important contribution in money during the Depression when we needed it the most," Pat later recalled. "She worked and contributed for a longer period of time than anyone else. She also spent much of her free time looking after the household and the younger children before she was married."

Care and feeding of her siblings. Constant moving from place to place. The pressures brought on by the Depression. School. Work. Church. Watching her brothers go off to war, and waiting for news when the young GIs were in trouble. Fran felt the strain of all of these responsibilities. Even after she married and had children of her own, she remained a vital touchstone when things went wrong in her mother's house.

Vincenza was hit by a train in 1940 and sustained serious injuries. The family doctor insisted that her legs could be saved, and he used metal plates and plaster casts to do just that.

"When Ma came home," Donald recalled, "we had to set up a hospital bed in the living room for her since her bedroom was upstairs and she was confined to bed for a long period of time." Eventually the casts came off, but Vincenza's legs were permanently misshapen.

Pat was a student at Niagara University at the time, and he learned about the accident during football practice. "I told Dad and Mom that I was going to quit Niagara and go to work under the circumstances," Pat recalled in 2001. "But they both said definitely not – since I was the only one so far that had gone to university."

Instead, Pat put his schooling to use by negotiating with the railroad for a cash settlement. To his dismay, his mother wanted the money right away and decided to settle quickly. Pat thought the family could do better.

Even with the settlement in hand, the whole family had to pitch in after the accident – including Frances, now a wife and mother living in her own house. "Everyone from Frances to Donald made efforts to contribute to the welfare of the family one way or another," recalled Pat.

*

Tony and Fran assumed a new role in 1961 when their first grandchild arrived on the scene. Eight more grandchildren followed in the next 14 years.

"When Julie was born, she was everything," says Frances. "We used to go just to see the baby."

Fran doted on every one of her grandchildren. She never missed a birthday or a family gathering. She babysat whenever she was needed. She had us over for sleepovers and attended our school functions. She was a constant presence for everyone lucky enough to call her "Grandma."

*

Of course, Grandma Frances was still a daughter – and her mother could be tough to please. Vincenza had lived for a number of years with Pat's family in Chicago, but she returned to Niagara Falls in the 1970s. After several moves, she settled into a high-rise building for older adults, where she lived independently in a comfortable apartment. Her daughter Evelyn lived down the hall, giving her an extra level of care and support. But that doesn't mean she was thrilled with the setup.

"She'd call my brothers up and tell them, 'They put me in jail and nobody cares about me,'" says Fran.

Vincenza was known for summoning multiple family members at the same time for the same chore. Three people would show up simultaneously with milk, because "Big Grandma," as she was known, had called every one of them to report that she was all out.

"One Thanksgiving, I asked her to come over and have dinner with us," says Fran, "but she said she wasn't going out because her boys would be calling her and she had to be home to answer their calls. Evelyn asked her, Jim asked her, but she wouldn't go to any of us. So (Eleanor's older daughter) Shirley decided she'd cook dinner and take it over there. She took the kids and brought a turkey, the whole meal, packed everything up and they had dinner all together.

Don called my mother to wish her a happy Thanksgiving, and she said, 'I all alone here. You have a good time? I all alone. Nobody come, nobody invite me.' Shirley got so mad, she went into the bedroom and picked up the phone and said, 'Donald, I'm here. I brought turkey and everything!'"

Privately, Fran would get exasperated with her mother. But she never stopped visiting her and caring for her needs. Family comes first.

The whole DeBiase family made an effort to stay connected across the miles. Frequent family reunions, not to mention phone calls and letters, kept the scattered clan together. "We've always been close," says Fran. "Everybody's always been there for everybody else, and they always kept in touch. I never knew when any minute one of my brothers would call, no matter where they lived."

*

Tony and Fran celebrated their 50th wedding anniversary in September 1985 with a Mass, party and family reunion in Niagara Falls. Relatives attended from all over for a joyful get-together. But storm clouds were gathering.

Frances was in the parking lot one night after church, talking with a friend. She assumed my grandfather had gone to get the car, as he usually did. But seconds turned to minutes, and he never reappeared. Cell phones were many years away, so Fran's friend offered to take her home. "I said no," Frances says with a laugh. "I'm going to wait! He's got to come back! And he did. He had gotten a few blocks and realized I wasn't in the car."

It was more than my grandfather's impatience that caused him to drive away that night. From time to time, he would complain of a foul odor that no one else could smell. He would zone out and have trouble standing or talking. Each of these episodes was a "mini-stroke." These incidents caused a continuous loss of memory and function.

Sometimes my grandfather left the house and didn't return for hours because he couldn't find his way home. One day he went out to the garage, got into his immaculate light blue Chevy Impala, put it into gear and tried to back out of the driveway. Unfortunately, he put the car in drive instead of reverse, and he drove through the back of the garage. Finally, the doctor told him he had to give up his car keys.

Because my grandmother had never learned to drive, the two of them became dependent on their family to transport them around town. "I can picture Mom standing on the porch under the light with folded arms when Vin and I were just a very few seconds late," says Marie.

I was just a kid when all of this happened, but my grandmother's choices made a lasting impact on me. Even though his condition made it difficult to care for him, Frances refused to admit my grandfather to a nursing home. Instead, she kept him at home for several years, with the help of various programs and agencies – and, of course, with the devoted help of her daughters.

It was a great sacrifice. In his later years, my grandfather barely made sense when he spoke. As his consciousness slipped away, he would sit for hours and grind his teeth, loudly and incessantly. Sometimes he wouldn't eat. He would spit out his medicine. When he went somewhere, even to a family birthday party, he would often sit in the car and refuse to get out. Then he started getting up during the night and planting himself on the stairs between the first and second floors of the house. His cognitive skills were diminished, but physically he was as strong as a horse. It would take two or three grandsons to move him.

Under the circumstances, my grandmother couldn't leave the house without having someone to stay with him. But there was never a question about keeping him at home.

My grandfather was a shadow of himself by the end of his life. He spent all day and night lying in bed, unaware of his surroundings. He didn't know anyone, not even his wife of 56 years. But he was home, and she felt that she had done right by him.

*

As a sister, an aunt, a mother, a grandmother and a wife, Frances has devoted herself to the needs of her family. Aunt Joyce was right. Frances always knew how to make everything better.

9

Don't Play Favorites

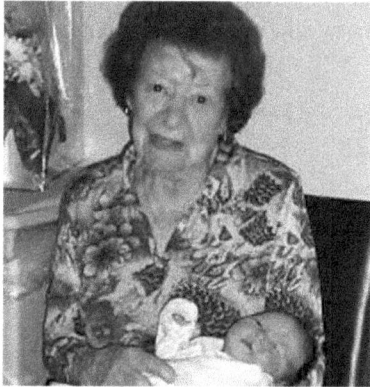

Frances holding great-granddaughter Katie Paterson

Frances treasured every one of her brothers and sisters, but she wasn't always happy when a new one arrived.

"One time when we were living in New Castle, I think when Lou was born, I complained about it," Frances remembers. "I said, 'There are too many kids here.' And my mother said, 'Do you want to get rid of them?' I said yes, so she said, 'Okay, which one should we get rid of?' And I couldn't think of any. I said, 'Oh no, not John. Oh no, not Pat.' And my mother said, 'Well, we better just keep 'em all.'"

*

Decades later, Fran went out of her way to treat every one of her grandchildren the same. She took pains to spend the same amount on everyone's birthday and Christmas gifts. She never praised or bragged about one grandchild more than another. What she did for one, she did for all. Nobody knew if she ever had a favorite. She would never have allowed it to show.

In a world filled with relationships soured by favoritism from parents and grandparents, I count myself blessed that Frances always dealt with us all so evenly.

I think my grandmother's equal treatment of everyone in the family is the reason that we don't have feuds, grudges and rivalries. Everyone has always felt loved and cared for. Without deep-seated resentments, we're all able to get along and look out for each other.

10

Think Before You Buy

Frances during the Depression, which shaped her financial habits

It's hard to believe nowadays, but in the 1980s you could actually make money on bank interest. Banks competed to win customers by promising high yields on certificates of deposit. Ever the savvy money manager, Frances Genovese was in on the action. She tracked the interest rates and moved her money around in an attempt to maximize her returns. And at any point, she could tell you where every account was located and exactly how much was in it.

*

A few months before their wedding, my grandparents went to a store called Mendelssohn's to look at furniture for the house they were preparing to move into. They picked out a bedroom set, a couch, chairs and a dining room set, all in one trip. Their furniture was selected, moved in and paid for by the time they got married in September.

"We got it all for $777," Fran recalls with remarkable precision.

There's something even more notable than the fact that my grandmother still remembers exactly what she paid for her furniture 80 years ago. What's really amazing is how long she kept the furniture. The dining room set survived for more than 65 years, until she moved into an apartment and had to downsize. The light blue couch and most of the bedroom set from 1935 remained in use until a few months ago.

My grandmother's brand of conservation mystifies much of my family. But the Great Depression survivor couldn't help thinking that her couch was still good and it would be silly to waste money on a new one. Ditto for the bedroom furniture, and for the dining room set that would still be around if only there were a dining room to house it.

Over the years, my grandmother has held on to coffeemakers, can openers and lots of other gadgets that were on their last legs. Why? Because they got the job done.

It's possible to take this kind of thing too far. There's nothing unreasonable about buying new furniture or new appliances from time to time. But my grandmother's mindset isn't a bad example for the profligate spenders of our time. To put it simply: don't waste your money. Think about whether you really need something before you buy it.

*

Frances saw both sides of the housing crisis that erupted in 2008. Sure, she thought the banks had been shifty in approving mortgages for people who couldn't afford them. But she also held the homeowners responsible. In her mind, it's not smart to take on debt that you can't afford. She couldn't figure out how homebuyers failed to do the math before making that kind of decision.

Likewise, she's dumbfounded by the credit card debt that folks carry these days. To someone who was formed by the harsh realities of the 1930s, it's really important to pay as you go. My grandmother will concede that a lot of personal debt happens because of bad luck. But she knows that some personal debt happens because of bad judgment. Frances believes that if you don't have the money in hand, you shouldn't buy the extras.

My grandparents bought their first car – a used car – in the early 1950s for the whopping price of $100. "My brother was talking to somebody who had a used car lot," Fran says. "The man said, 'I have

86

something here that isn't that good looking, but it runs.' So my brother came over and told us to look at it, and that's how we ended up with our first car."

That's all they wanted – a car that ran.

Before they bought that first car, they took buses and they walked. After they bought the car, my grandmother still took buses and walked, because my grandfather used the car to go back and forth to his job. There were five people in the house and one car for all of them. They made it work.

There's a big difference between today's "necessities" and the necessities of my grandmother's generation. Back then, milk and bread were necessities; even butter was a treat while rationing was going on. A television set and a private phone line were niceties that people bought when they were sure they could afford them. A car was a luxury.

Today's 9-year-olds have TVs in their rooms and iPhones in their hands. High school students drive cars that are nicer than the ones my parents drove when they were in their 30s with kids of their own.

Sure, times have changed. Consumer products are more accessible and affordable than before, and failure to keep up with technology can make us less productive as students and less marketable as workers. Most of our communities are not very walkable, so cars are more of a necessity than they used to be. But we can still learn a thing or two from the frugality of my grandmother's generation.

We should be aware of what we have in the bank and what we can afford. Before we buy something, we should stop and think about whether it's worth it. And we should be very careful about taking on new debt. That's just common sense, Frances style.

11

Don't Let Anyone Else Define You

Frances celebrating her 104th birthday

My grandmother was diagnosed with carpal tunnel syndrome and had to have surgery on her hand when she was in her early 90s. She quickly became a sentimental favorite of the medical staff.

A nurse, who was Italian American, looked at Frances's chart and did a double-take. (We're all used to the double-take. No one can believe that my grandmother is as old as she is.)

"You don't look that old," the nurse said.

"Well, I am," Frances replied.

Then the nurse told my grandmother that she'd have to take her teeth out before the surgery. My grandmother replied, "I don't have false teeth."

The nurse yelled, "Mamma mia!" and the whole office burst out laughing.

*

Surprise is the first element of breaking down stereotypes. Stereotypes are nothing more than shallow assumptions: if you look like this, it must mean that you'll behave in this way. Racism and sexism are broken when people defy the narrow expectations that are placed on them.

So is ageism. In our youth-obsessed culture, many of us recoil from the aging process. It reminds us of the inevitable path that all of us are traveling. No one likes to look mortality in the eye.

We need examples of successful aging. We need to see that it's possible to grow older without growing bitter or feeble. My grandmother used to resist being one of those examples. Well into her 90s, she really didn't want people to know her age. But she learned to embrace it at some point and began to relish the opportunity to shatter stereotypes.

She has chosen to remain as active as possible. She has always dressed well. She knows what's happening in the life of every grandchild and great-grandchild, and she enjoys telling stories about each one's latest exploits. "They're all precious," she says, "every one of them."

She acts as if her age is no big deal when people make a fuss about it. But her smile suggests she's having fun teaching other people a thing or two about aging.

*

More than four million Italian immigrants came to the United States between 1880 and 1920 in search of a better life. My great-grandparents were among them. They took nothing for granted – they knew they would have to work hard in America. But I wonder if they understood the hatred that awaited them on our shores.

Italian Americans were willing to work their way up the economic ladder by taking low-paying, menial jobs. Because of this, many Americans tagged these industrious newcomers as intellectually inferior brutes. Some Italian Americans, disillusioned by economic conditions in the old country, came to the United States espousing socialism and radicalism; as a result, Italian Americans were often unfairly branded as rabble-rousers. Then there was organized crime, a phenomenon through which a tiny minority of Italian Americans scarred the rest with images of violence and ruthlessness.

Thousands of Italian Americans were imprisoned by their own government during World War II. Thousands more were categorized as "resident aliens" and saw their civil liberties curtailed. The mainstream culture questioned where the loyalties of Italian Americans lay – with the pope, the motherland, or the United States. Despite all of this doubt – perhaps in part because of it – 1.2 million Italian Americans served in the armed forces during the war. Many more worked their fingers to the bone on the home front to hold their families and the country together.

In postwar America, Italian Americans took on ever greater roles in government, business, sports and entertainment. No one questions our loyalty anymore. Italian Americans now boast a higher high school and college graduation rate than the country as a whole. From those dark days of discrimination, Italian Americans have risen to become admired and even loved – all because millions of people like Frances Genovese said "no" to the small-minded stereotypes of their time and taught us to do the same.

My grandmother and her brothers and sisters never looked down on those who did manual labor – they had all done manual labor themselves. But they pushed us to seek education, speak well and carry ourselves with dignity. And the Mafia culture was never glorified in our family – we quickly learned that crime was not part of our legacy or our destiny. By the way they conducted themselves, Frances and her generation instilled pride in all the best of the Italian American culture – hospitality, community, family and faith – while simultaneously rejecting those typecasts that threatened to drag all of us down.

My grandmother never said these words to me, but the message runs through her whole life: you're the only one who can decide what kind of person you're going to be. If you don't like the path that has been set for you, go out and change it.

12

It's Never the
Wrong Time to Laugh

Frances cutting up with her daughter Joan

Once, my mother and grandmother were walking into a funeral home. My mother noticed a mark that resembled a bullet hole on the front door. She turned to my grandmother and said, "Who would shoot at a funeral home?"

Frances replied, "Maybe somebody was trying to get out," causing my mother to break up laughing just as she opened the door and walked into a hallway filled with mourners.

*

My brother, Bill, hates clutter and tries not to accumulate stuff. He used to joke that he had to discard something old whenever he got something new. Someone would buy him a pair of socks for his birthday, and he'd throw out an old pair to make room. One year on his birthday, my grandmother gave him a card with money in it, along with a note that said, "I'd like to see you throw the old one away."

That's her sense of humor.

But my grandmother has taught us more than the value of a good laugh. She has taught us that it's OK to laugh even when it might seem inappropriate. She understands that a well-timed one-liner can relieve pressure and make a tough moment easier. That ability to laugh at the absurdity of life came from her dad.

"He was serious, but he was comical," she says. To hear Frances tell it, her mother didn't exactly appreciate Donato's playfulness – especially when it was directed at other women, no matter how innocently. But Donato got the last laugh – literally.

One particular female friend of the family was often on the receiving end of Donato's good-natured teasing. For whatever reason, this poor lady couldn't keep her stockings from drooping. She was forever pulling them up, and Donato delighted in pointing it out. When Donato died, this same lady attended the wake. She knelt in front of the casket to say a prayer, and when she got up, her stockings fell and she reached down to pull them up.

There, during one of the saddest moments of her life, my grandmother fell apart laughing. Her whole family looked at her like she was crazy, but she knew she was sharing one more laugh with her father.

*

Even my grandmother's childhood pastor, Father Nicolo DeMita, showed a sense of humor at Mass. "I've never known a priest as compassionate," she says. "Any family that needed anything, he was sure to bring them something and do something for them. But he also had a comical side. I remember one time, when he was giving the sermon, he said, 'All you women, before you come to church, wash your hands. By the time the 12:00 Mass is done, the holy water smells like garlic!'"

*

Frances turned her sharp wit on herself in October 2005. She fell in her apartment one Saturday afternoon while getting ready for church. The result: a fractured hip. I was supposed to take her to Mass that day, but when I reached her apartment, I saw an ambulance pulling away. My mother met me in the parking lot and told me what had happened. Being the organist, I still had to go to church. So I sat through Mass, trying to play and sing, but all I could think about was my grandmother.

I raced out of church after Mass and rushed to the emergency room. And what did I see? There was Frances, lying on a hospital bed and cracking jokes. She and my mother were filling out the admissions form and laughing their heads off. Frances wanted to answer "yes" to the question "Are you pregnant or nursing?"

"I just want to see what they would say," she giggled.

This happened the weekend of Halloween. She went through surgery and rehab, and was back home for Thanksgiving. If we needed proof that a sense of humor really does help, there it is.

13

This Too Shall Pass

Frances dancing the Tarantella with son-in-law Vin Chiarenza

My grandmother underwent a hip replacement at age 97. Obviously we were concerned. Her own mother had died at age 93 after falling and breaking her hip. We had to wonder if this could be the beginning of the end for Frances.

But the surgery went well, and she was discharged to a nursing home for rehab after a few days in the hospital. She absolutely hated rehab. She just wanted to go home.

I took Communion to Frances every Saturday night while she was in rehab. I got there a few minutes late one night, and she had already gone to the dining room. When I walked in, I saw her sitting at the table, slumped over in a wheelchair looking dejected. It was one of the most heartbreaking sights I've ever seen. Just then, she looked up and spotted me. She gave me a wan smile and a timid wave, almost like a kid who's picked up at summer camp after being left against her will.

Some people would have been defeated by that experience, but not Frances. No, she used it as motivation. She pushed herself through physical therapy in record time and forced herself to get better, because she knew that was the only way she could go home.

"I never said, 'Oh, I want to die, I have to have an operation,'" she says. "I never wanted to die. If it happens, it happens, but I'm not going to pray for it. I'm not going to look forward to it!"

*

My grandmother always had a favorite phrase, one that my mother heard so many times as a kid that it still echoes in her mind: "This too shall pass." Frances was never one for self-pity. She was optimistic enough to believe that things would get better.

She refused to wallow even when she landed in the hospital with congestive heart failure at 102. She didn't like the situation, obviously, but she was the first to acknowledge that other people were worse off.

*

I have seen my grandmother cry three times. The first time was at the funeral home when my grandfather died. Frances sobbed for a minute when she saw the body in the casket for the first time. Then she stiffened her spine, put on a brave face, and greeted callers with poise and dignity for two days.

A few weeks later, she invited all of the grandchildren over to her home. She started to tell us that she and my grandfather had saved so that they could give us all a small inheritance. But she couldn't finish the sentence. She started to cry. After a few seconds, she pulled herself together and distributed the envelopes. It was 11 years before I saw her cry again.

My Uncle Vin Chiarenza died of cancer in 2002. He was my Aunt Marie's husband and Frances's first son-in-law. He was funny, generous and kind – one of the rocks of our family. Because I was a pall bearer, I saw my grandmother say her last goodbye. She broke down and cried, having lost the son-in-law who had treated her like his own mother and danced the Tarantella with her at so many family weddings.

The hurt continued after the funeral. But Frances didn't cry again, at least not in front of us. Aunt Marie, too, carried on with remarkable strength. My Aunt Anne showed the same resilience 18 years earlier when she lost her husband, Bill, at a very young age. And my mom kept a stiff upper lip and stayed composed when my dad had successful open-heart surgery in 2008.

The women in my family understand that in a moment of crisis or tragedy, decisions have to be made and life has to move forward – and they are able to stay clear-eyed enough to take care of things. Sure, they experience emotion – but they don't let themselves break, because there's work to do. They hold themselves together – and in the process they hold us together, too.

*

I once had to take an online personality assessment as part of a job interview. According to my profile, one of my strongest attributes is my response time. I don't need a lot of time to react and collect my thoughts when something bad happens. I just deal with it. It's fine to be sad, but it's not fine to be paralyzed. This too shall pass.

I attribute that resilience to my grandmother and my mother. I was raised to accept that not everything in life will go my way, and I can't let myself get mired in sadness or regret or bitterness when I don't get what I want. Life moves in one direction. Sometimes you just have to pick yourself up, dust yourself off and move on.

14

Put All the Pieces Together

Frances (at the bottom of the ladder) painting the house

My grandfather never lost at the track. At least he never admitted it. He'd brag about it when he won. Otherwise, he'd say he broke even.

One of my grandfather's cousins pulled me aside when I was a teenager. "You know," he told me, "you're very lucky to have your grandmother. Your grandfather was sure lucky to have her. He liked to bet at the racetrack. But your grandmother kept control of the accounts, and she had money hidden in places he never knew about. She managed their money very well."

Whenever I think of that story, I'm reminded of a great scene from the movie "My Big Fat Greek Wedding." Maria Portokalos, played perfectly by Lainie Kazan, is preparing to convince her husband to let their daughter go to college. The daughter, Toula, says, "Ma, Dad is so stubborn. What he says, goes. 'Ah, the man is the head of the house.'"

Maria responds, "The man may be the head, but the woman is the neck – and she can move the head any way she wants."

106

Maria's genius lies in the fact that she wins her husband to her side by convincing him that it's his idea. She lets him believe he's in charge, even though the audience can clearly see that she's pulling the strings.

I think that's how it was with my grandmother. My grandfather rose and slept every single day believing he was firmly in control of his household. In reality, my grandmother had at least as much to say about what happened. But she let him think what he needed to think because of the era and the cultural dynamics that shaped their relationship.

*

My grandmother was no shrinking violet. She worked outside the home in a time when many of her contemporaries didn't. She formed her own opinions, earned money, made good financial decisions, and did things around the house. One of my favorite pictures is of my grandmother, standing on the roof of the porch on 63rd Street, painting the house.

At the same time, she dressed nicely, cooked, cleaned and read bedtime stories. Frances was, and is, a complete person.

In looking beyond traditional gender roles, my grandmother was ahead of her time. These days, many husbands and wives share duties that used to belong exclusively to one or the other.

It's that way in our house.

My wife and I still talk about something that happened not long after we started dating. While I was cooking dinner, the kitchen sink backed up. I was all set to call a plumber when Michele asked me in the most matter-of-fact way possible why I didn't just remove something called a "p-trap" and clear out the blockage. I stared back at her blankly, prompting her to don a pair of rubber gloves and fix the plumbing problem herself. Meanwhile, I kept cooking dinner.

That's how we are to this day. We pick up each other's slack. I do lots of "dad things" and my wife does lots of "mom things." But I'm not afraid to cook and clean and change diapers, and she's perfectly comfortable cutting grass and taking out the garbage and fixing things. Today's hectic family life requires everyone to pitch in.

*

The lesson I've drawn from Frances is that we shouldn't be afraid to step outside the roles that society hands to us. Most people aren't the one-dimensional characters that we see in sitcoms. A woman is more than a nagging shopaholic, and a man is more than a clueless workaholic. It's okay for us to be complex, to put all of the pieces together that have been given to us.

For many years, one of the fixtures in my grandmother's kitchen was a little plaque that read, "Women have many faults, men only two: everything they say and do." That's about as much as my grandmother has ever had to say about gender.

She didn't need to say anything. She just did whatever had to be done – and in the process, she showed us everything a well-rounded woman is capable of.

15

The Last Chapter
Isn't the Whole Story

Her recent health struggles don't erase Frances's remarkable life story

In 2010, home care aides began visiting my grandmother twice a week to help her prepare meals, clean her apartment and get in and out of the shower. This wasn't an expense that my grandmother appreciated, nor was it a service she particularly wanted. She would often say that she didn't think she really needed an aide twice a week, that she could do everything for herself, and that she was thinking about cutting her hours.

That changed when Frances fell again in July 2011 and broke her other hip. The surgeon gave her two options: take the risk of surgery and face possible death on the operating table, or go without the surgery and remain bedridden. Congestive heart failure had taken its toll by this point. She was nowhere near as strong as she had been when she faced hip surgery six years earlier.

She made her decision quickly. She could handle the risk of death, but she couldn't stand the thought of spending the rest of her life in bed, in pain and unable to walk. She chose surgery. It went as well as it could have. Only later did we learn that even my grandmother's physician didn't think Frances would survive the operation.

After surgery, my grandmother spent several difficult weeks in rehab. Most of us expected the rehab facility to recommend admitting her into skilled nursing. But that didn't happen. Frances was compromised, but not enough to stay in the nursing home. Still, it was clear that she was going to need a lot more help if she was still going to live at home.

I had been working for seven years to bring a national model called the Program of All-Inclusive Care for the Elderly to Niagara Falls. This program provides all the medical and social services needed to keep frail elders living at home instead of going into nursing homes. My grandmother used to tell me she would be the first person to sign up.

It took a lot longer to start the program than we expected. It finally opened in September 2011, at the very moment that my grandmother was being released from rehab. And sure enough, she became the first to enroll. The program became a lifeline for Frances, providing physical therapy, clinical services, transportation, medical oversight and a daily trip to the center for socialization.

With the opening of the PACE program behind me, I decided it was time for a new job. But before I began my next career adventure, I worked on site for four months at the day center that Frances was visiting every day. I quickly learned that she expected me to drop by on a daily basis. If I forgot, or if I missed her because of my schedule, she would send someone to my office to say that she was looking for me. So I got into the habit of visiting every day, and I loved the time I was able to spend with her as she settled into the program.

*

Frances was no longer reading as voraciously as she always had. She was less insistent on being at holidays and family gatherings. As it became harder for her to go out, she was more likely to sit in her chair in front of the television.

Sometimes it seemed that my grandmother was losing some of her pep. And yet, she pushed herself to attend our wedding in November 2011, and she balked at those in the family who said she had to choose between the church and the reception. She went to both. We arranged to have a wheelchair van pick her up at the reception site and take her back home. She got home at 9:30 that night – well past her usual bedtime – but afterward she told everyone who would listen that she would have liked to stay longer.

Some of the old fire was still there.

Not long before Frances's 104th birthday, my brother heard her say, "I'm not ready to give up yet."

*

Frances's slow decline has been tough on her daughters, who have worked tirelessly to see that her every need is met. They have all had to concede that their mother isn't the same person she used to be. At her age, who would be?

It seems unfair for someone to make it so long with good health and a positive outlook, only to slip at the end. It's almost like fumbling the ball at the 5-yard line. And yet, without intending to, my grandmother has taught us one more lesson in all of this. She has shown us that the final chapter isn't the whole story – that we can't judge the totality of a life only by what happens at the end.

My grandmother is still an extraordinary person with a remarkable story. Her legacy is secure, no matter what happens now. None of these recent, difficult moments can erase more than 100 years of grace, compassion and kindness.

Someday – and I've long since given up making predictions when it comes to my grandmother's longevity – Frances Genovese will meet her Maker. The body of work that she'll take with her is a life overwhelmingly well-lived. We have all of these life lessons to prove it.

Epilogue

Frances at 104, holding Will and adjusting to a new way of life

The day our son was born, Frances called my mother looking for details. She went to the day center and reported to her friends on the baby's name, height and length. Michele and I were planning to take Will for a visit to Frances's apartment as soon as possible – maybe even on the way home from the hospital.

We never got the chance.

Frances fell at home and broke her pelvis the day after Will was born. She was admitted to the hospital – unfortunately, not the same one that we were in – and was quickly discharged to the nursing home for rehab. Unable to walk without assistance, she began a grueling regimen of physical and occupational therapy.

We asked the pediatrician if we could take Will to visit his great-grandmother in the nursing home. The doctor said he normally wouldn't advise that kind of visit for at least a month, but under the circumstances he told us to go as soon as possible. "If she's 104," the doctor said, "you don't want to take any chances. It will be good for all of you to make the visit." We did – and it was.

117

My mother and her sisters were exhausted at this point. They had all done their share of caregiving, and it was getting harder for them to meet Frances's growing needs. They thought it best for her to stay in the nursing home permanently. But my grandmother was sure she could keep doing the things she had always done, with a little extra help.

I had fought like hell to keep her at home a year earlier, because I didn't think she was ready for the nursing home. This time around, even I had to admit that she wasn't safe living on her own anymore, no matter how many aides might be assigned to her. She simply needed a higher level of care.

A delicate dance took place for a few weeks among Frances, her daughters and her care team. As the therapists marveled at the progress she was making, it looked at times as if she might be sent home. But she still couldn't walk or do much of anything else without a lot of help. None of us could see how would be able to live in her apartment, even with 24-hour care.

Physical therapy became more grueling as the weeks went by, and my grandmother began to realize that this time was different. When her daughters would ask her how she was going to take care of herself, she would acknowledge that she couldn't. Granted, minutes later she would say she wanted to go home. But deep down, reality was sinking in.

Before long, she was moved to a new room on another floor. She was now close to the chapel and started attending Mass on a regular basis. There was more happening on this floor, so Frances saw new opportunities for socialization and activity. She began to talk about giving up her apartment, furniture and belongings.

The day finally came when the care team sat alone in a room with my grandmother, with no other family present. When she was asked what she wanted to do, she said, "I can't go home." And with that, Frances became a permanent resident of the nursing home.

Frances visited my parents' house on Thanksgiving 2012 and had dinner with us. Her brother Donald called from Las Vegas to wish her a happy Thanksgiving. I overheard her talking with him about her new home. "They treat me really well," she told him, "and I have everything I need. I'm in the right place."

With the help of a wheelchair van, she gets out for major holidays, and she still visits the PACE center two days a week for socialization.

And of course, she has a steady stream of visitors. Her family now totals 35 – including her three daughters, her son-in-law, her nine grandchildren and their seven spouses, and her 14 great-grandchildren plus one fiancé.

Sure, she sometimes makes comments about wanting to leave the nursing home. But for the most part, she has come to terms with the situation. She doesn't make anybody feel guilty about the fact that she's there. She is making the best of it.

*

It wasn't easy for Frances to accept living in a skilled nursing facility. For years she had said, "Whatever happens, I just don't want to go to a nursing home." I never imagined that, at 104, she would rethink this position.

But maybe it's not so shocking. Frances has always refused to just stand there. She has never been so rigid in her thinking that she couldn't evolve with the times. At 104, she still had the capacity to face the future with confidence instead of living in the past. When her circumstances changed, ultimately she changed with them. Maybe that's the best lesson of all.

She is very much holding her own as she approaches 105 – enjoying time with family and friends, telling stories, and adjusting to whatever life has in store for her. Frances Genovese may be in a wheelchair, but she's not sitting still.

About the Author

Frances with the author on his wedding day in 2011

Jeff Paterson is executive director of Community Music School of Buffalo, New York, and a faculty member at the State University College of New York at Buffalo.

A church musician since the age of 12, he earned a master's degree in pastoral ministry from Christ the King Seminary in Buffalo. He serves as a pastoral musician at St. John de LaSalle Roman Catholic Church in Niagara Falls, where four generations of his family have worshiped.

Jeff lives in Niagara Falls, New York, with his wife, Michele, and their son, Will.

www.ingramcontent.com/pod-product-compliance
Lightning Source LLC
Chambersburg PA
CBHW050354280326
41933CB00010BA/1459